OUR GOVERNMENT

VOTING IN ELECTIONS

BY JACK MANNING

I Voted

CAPSTONE PRESS
a capstone imprint

First Facts are published by Capstone Press,
1710 Roe Crest Drive, North Mankato, Minnesota 56003
www.capstonepub.com

Library of Congress Cataloging-in-Publication Data
Cataloging information on file with the Library of Congress
ISBN 978-1-4914-0334-1 (library binding)
ISBN 978-1-4914-0338-9 (paperback)
ISBN 978-1-4914-0342-6 (eBook PDF)

Editorial Credits
Brenda Haugen, editor; Heidi Thompson, designer; Eric Gohl, media researcher;
Katy LaVigne, production specialist

Photo Credits
Dreamstime: Jennifer Pitiquen, 13, Jinlide, 1, Joshua Haviv, 19; iStockphotos: EdStock, 5; Library of Congress: 9, 11; Newscom: ZUMA Press/The Washington Times, 21; Shutterstock: Chris Parypa Photography, cover (background), Ken Wolter, cover (stickers), Lisa F. Young, 17, Paul Hakimata Photography, 7, Spirit of America, 15; SuperStock: Blend Images, cover

Printed in China by Nordica
0414/CA21400593
032014   008095NORDF14

TABLE OF CONTENTS

CHAPTER 1

THE RIGHT TO VOTE

People in the United States are able to make many choices. Using their right to **vote** is one of the most important choices they can make.

The U.S. government is a **republic**. It is based on the **Constitution** and is called a **democracy**. People have the right to choose leaders. Voting gives people a voice in government.

vote—to make a choice in an election
republic—a kind of government in which the people elect a small group to make decisions for the whole
Constitution—the written system of laws in the United States; it states the rights of the people and the powers of government
democracy—a government in which people choose their leaders by voting

CHAPTER 2

PEOPLE ELECT LEADERS

Citizens vote for leaders for national, state, and city governments. Most leaders serve **terms** that last two, four, or six years.

People choose a president every four years in the United States. The president leads the whole country.

citizen—a member of a country, state, or city who has the right to live there
term—a set period of time that elected leaders serve in office

CHAPTER 3

VOTING HISTORY

Can you imagine being told you could not vote because of the color of your skin? Or because you were a woman? Years ago only white men who owned land could vote. Some people believed this was not fair.

For years many people
worked hard to win voting rights.
African-American men finally
won the right to vote in 1870.
It took another 50 years before
all women won voting rights.

 **FACT** Women who owned a certain amount of property could vote in New Jersey in 1776.

African-American men voting for the first time

CHAPTER 4

WHO CAN VOTE?

How do you know if you can vote? The U.S. government and the states make rules for voters. Today people must be U.S. citizens to vote. They must be at least 18 years old. In most states citizens must **register** to vote.

FACT North Dakota is the only U.S. state where people don't have to register to vote.

register—to enter a voter's name on an official list

CHAPTER 5

INFORMED VOTERS

Before voting, people learn about the **candidates** and the **issues**. They listen to candidates' plans and ideas. Citizens vote for the candidates they feel will do the best job. Learning about candidates and the issues helps people choose good leaders.

FACT In the United States, most voters learn about candidates from TV, newspapers, and the Internet.

candidate—a person who runs for office, such as president
issue—an idea or need that is talked about by citizens and government leaders

15

CHAPTER 6

WHERE CITIZENS VOTE

Citizens vote at **polling places** on **Election** Day. Schools, city halls, fire stations, and other public buildings can be polling places.

Workers at polling places make sure people are registered to vote. They hand out **ballots**. They also make sure each person votes only one time. Some workers volunteer to help at polling places for free. Others are paid for their work.

polling place—the place where people vote in an election
election—the process of choosing someone or deciding something by voting
ballot—a punch card, piece of paper, or electronic screen on which a person's vote is recorded

FACT People have voted in chocolate shops, bowling alleys, and hair salons in Chicago, Illinois.

CHAPTER 7

HOW CITIZENS VOTE

When voting, citizens enter private booths with ballots. A ballot lists all the candidates in the election. People vote by marking the ballots near the names of the candidates.

Some voters can't go to polling places. They mail in **absentee** ballots instead.

absentee—given by someone who is not present

CHAPTER 8

COUNTING VOTES

When the election is done, the votes are counted. Votes can be counted by hand. Some places also use computers to count votes. In all elections except for U.S. president, the person with the most votes is the winner.

Amazing but True!

Did you know that a candidate for U.S. president can get the most votes but still lose the election? It's true! The president is actually chosen by the 538 members of the Electoral College called electors. States with more people have more electors than states with fewer people. The candidate who gets the most citizen votes usually wins all of the Electoral College votes from that state. In a close election, a candidate can lose the citizen vote but become president by winning the most electoral votes.

Team 14

FACT A difference of just one vote decided the 1839 governor's race in Massachusetts.

GLOSSARY

absentee (AB-suhn-tee)—given by someone who is not present

ballot (BAL-uht)—a punch card, piece of paper, or electronic screen on which a person's vote is recorded

candidate (KAN-di-date)—a person who runs for office, such as president

citizen (SIT-i-zuhn)—a member of a country, state, or city who has the right to live there

Constitution (con-stuh-TOO-shuhn)—the written system of laws in the United States; it states the rights of the people and the powers of government

democracy (di-MOK-ruh-see)—a government in which people choose their leaders by voting

election (i-LEK-shuhn)—the process of choosing someone or deciding something by voting

issue (ISH-yoo)—an idea or need that is talked about by citizens and government leaders

polling place (POHL-ing PLAYSS)—the place where people vote in an election

register (REJ-uh-stur)—to enter a voter's name on an official list

republic (ri-PUHB-lik)—a kind of government in which the people elect a small group to make decisions for the whole

term (TERM)—a set period of time that elected leaders serve in office

vote (VOHT)—to make a choice in an election

READ MORE

Peppas, Lynn. *Election Day*. Celebrations in My World. New York: Crabtree Pub. Co., 2010.

Rissman, Rebecca. *Election Day*. Holidays and Festivals. Chicago: Heinemann Library, 2011.

Sobel, Syl. *How the U.S. Government Works*. Hauppauge, N.Y.: Barrons Educational Series, Inc., 2012.

INTERNET SITES

FactHound offers a safe, fun way to find Internet sites related to this book. All of the sites on FactHound have been researched by our staff.

Here's all you do:

Visit *www.facthound.com*

Type in this code: 9781491403341

Super-cool stuff! Check out projects, games and lots more at
www.capstonekids.com

INDEX

CRITICAL THINKING USING THE COMMON CORE

1. Who can vote in elections? Do they have to do anything special to be able to vote? (Key Ideas and Details)
2. Candidates talk about issues during an election. If you were a candidate to lead your city or state, what issues would you talk about? Say why. (Integration of Knowledge and Ideas)